The Day of the Dead : *Día de los Muertos*

Virgin of Soledad
Mural, Oaxaca

The Day of the Dead

Día de los Muertos

PHOTOGRAPHS BY *Denis Defibaugh*

TEXT BY *Ward S. Albro*

 TCU Press
Fort Worth

LIBRARY OF CONGRESS CATALOGING-IN-PUBLICATION DATA

Albro, Ward S.
Day of the Dead / photographs by Denis Defibaugh; text by Ward Albro.
p. cm.
ISBN 978-0-87565-349-5 (alk. paper)
I. All Souls' Day—Mexico—Oaxaca de Juárez. 2. All Souls'
Day—Mexico—Oaxaca de Juárez—Pictorial works. 3. Oaxaca de Juárez
(Mexico)—Social life and customs. 4. Oaxaca de Juárez (Mexico)—Social life
and customs—Pictorial works. I. Defibaugh, Denis. II. Title.

GT4995.A4A524 2007
394.266—dc22

2006102971

Printed in China

FIRST EDITION

DEDICATED TO THE PEOPLE OF OAXACA

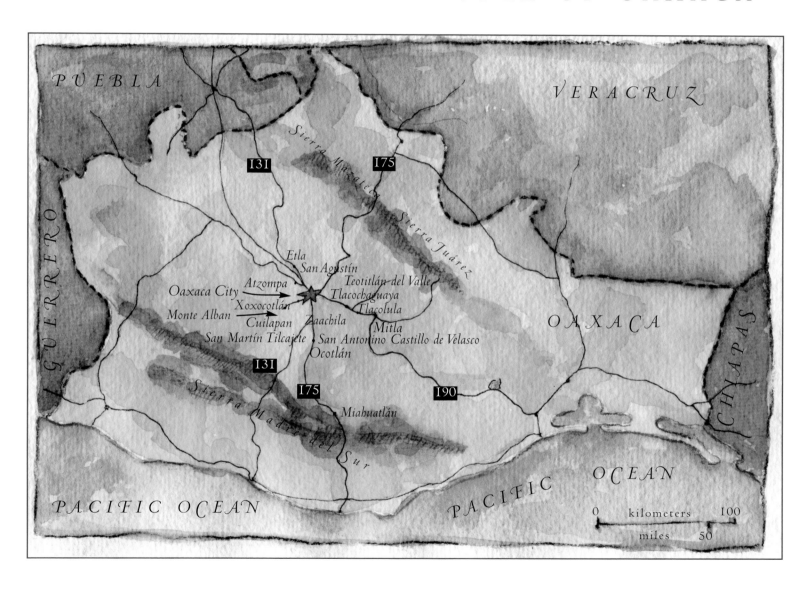

Etla *Comparsas,*
Last Rites

CONTENTS

Storyteller, Narciso
Hernández Luis,
Mitla

PREFACE

SIX A.M. WARD, PEDRO AND I ARE visiting with Narciso Hernandez Luis in Mitla, Oaxaca, known as the city of the dead. We eat *pan de muertos* and drink hot chocolate while Narciso describes meeting his departed brother at the family *ofrenda* on All Souls Day. As Narciso spoke, I noticed the morning sunlight illuminate the passageway to his home. In homage to his brother I asked Narciso to stand at the sun-drenched door so I could take his picture in that ethereal light. This portrait began my ongoing collaboration with the people of Oaxaca to document the community and events of Oaxaca's Day of the Dead—*Día de los Muertos.*

It is said every person's story is written plainly on his or her face, though not everyone can read it. My approach to documentary photography is to use the inherent qualities of photography, its ability to record with fidelity and detail. My photographs tell individual stories from the *Día de los Muertos* in Oaxaca. I have been photographing the *Muertos* in Oaxaca since 1994 when I received a grant from the Texas Committee for the Humanities to produce the "Family Ties Do Not Die: the *Día de los Muertos* in Oaxaca" project. In the past nine years I have been invited and inspired by the people of Oaxaca to photograph their personal celebration of the Day of the Dead. Early in the project I was reassured and encouraged to photograph when a family at the Atzompa cemetery perceived my presence (as a stranger in the cemetery) as being representative of spirits returning to the *Muertos* celebration.

Despite its popular appeal, The Day of the Dead in Oaxaca remains a traditional holiday. It is primarily a special time for families to come together to honor their *antepasados*, the family members who have died and whose spirits return to visit during these magical days. Throughout the state of Oaxaca, no other time of year is as important as the time of the *Muertos*.

The *Día de los Muertos* photographs attempt to express the joy, sorrow, and ritual of the many public celebrations of the *Muertos* and to capture the essence of the people, altars, crafts, and festivities of Oaxaca during the *Muertos* celebration.

When I first photographed the *Día de los Muertos*, I was impressed with the home and public altars. Each family altar was lovingly created in a prominent place, all in homage to a departed loved one, and each is decorated with a great variety of ornamentation and food that sits on and around the altars. Sugar cane, peanuts, fruit, *mole, mescal,* Coke, bread, sugar skulls, and flowers for the *Muertos* are found on many altars. Poor families have very modest altars, but they still provide

tribute to their ancestors. Each family has its own personal approach to decorating each year. Wood carvers have *animales* around their altars, public stores and markets display pottery, masks, papier mâché and arts from Oaxaca's famous artisans. I've been fortunate enough to be invited into a number of homes and asked to partake of this wonderful family tradition. By participating in eating, drinking, music, and friendship you become part of welcoming home the deceased loved ones and honoring their life and afterlife. It is also a custom to leave drinks, like the special *mescal* and chocolate on the altar and not drink these offerings until the actual celebration on the evening of November 1st. It is bad luck to take food and drink from the altar until the ancestors have arrived. An invited guest is offered much food and drink during a visit. On one occasion while visiting a home in Oaxaca, my writing companion, Ward Albro, and I vowed to not indulge in *mescal* before 11:00 A.M. After being offered *mescal* many times that morning we finally indulged and vowed not to drink before 9:00 A.M. It is impolite to refuse your host's offer of a taste at any time. I also remember an incident when my wife Elaine, who is a vegetarian, was invited to eat tamales. She said she didn't eat meat and

Zombies in Panteón, San
Antonino Castillo
de Velasco

Etla *Comparsas,* Cone head

politely was told that she could take the chicken out of the tamale. On each trip to Oaxaca I return with portraits for everyone whom I photographed during my previous visit. When I presented a print to a woman whom I photographed the year before, she excitedly remarked, "I didn't like having my picture taken at the time, but now I am glad I did." In the San Antonino cemetery, after I had given out all of the prints that I had with me, an elderly woman approached. Elvira, as she introduced herself, wanted to know where her portrait was. Inadvertently, I had not made one for her and apologized. I told her that I would return with her picture next year. To ensure my return, Elvira said in a quiet, yet stern voice, "If you don't give me my photograph, I will put a curse on you." Needless to say, as soon as I returned to Rochester, I made a print for her and put it in the mail.

My photographs from this project have been exhibited in museums, cultural centers, and universities. An exhibition at Rochester Institute of Technology, where I'm a professor in the School Photographic Arts and Sciences, enabled me to create an installation that stayed as true to tradition as possible. Accompanying the images was an altar decorated with the flow-ers of the *Muertos:* marigolds, lilies, and coxcomb. A local bakery recreated the famous *pan de muertos* for the altar. Traditional artisan crafts decorated the altar and gallery walls. An artist friend from Oaxaca, Antonio Cruz Zavaleta, created several sand paintings for the exhibition. During the evening of the opening my wife Elaine and a group of two hundred students constructed a large sand painting that was illuminated by a ring of candles. This artwork is akin to the installations near Oaxaca's cathedral each year. The opening began with a procession led by a musical group that played traditional music of Oaxaca.

One of my favorite photographs from this exhibition is of a proud candle maker named Biviana, who is just shy of five feet. In this image she is surrounded by the candles she made for a special altar. Her candles well exceeded her height. I was fortunate enough to spend several hours with Biviana as she shared her craft with me. She showed me how she made the candles' wax flowers and decorated them with gold ribbon. Biviana felt honored in her role as a candle maker for the *Días de los Muertos.* Over the course of three hours I photographed her making candles, inhaling smoke from an open fire, melting wax and working it into flower molds. At the end, a tired Biviana turned to me and said, "You owe me a Coke!"

I had many rich experiences with the people of Oaxaca while photographing throughout the past nine years. Images that come to mind include a black-and-white photograph of an adolescent girl sucking her thumb with her arms intertwined with those of her brother in front of their father's booth where traditional Halloween masks were sold. These masks were in sharp contrast to traditional wooden masks: plastic, rubberized personages of popular figures such as President and Mrs. Clinton, Laurel and Hardy, and President Salinas were on display. A panoramic view depicts a Catholic priest blessing vendor's stalls of *pan de muertos,* sugar skulls, candles, and trinkets being sold for the Day of the Dead. While the Catholic Church once held the Day of the Dead to be a pagan ritual, today it validates its historical, cultural, and communal importance.

Each of us has his own favorite place or event that we like to visit or participate in. The ritual and festivities of the *comparsas* or street theater have become my special subject to photograph. The *comparsas* is a community event for each barrio.

Initially the performance is comprised of a man near death, his wife, the devil, a priest, death, and a doctor. All are trying to save or gain his soul. Each actor presents a few lines to suggest his desire for the soul of the man. In addition, jokes and quips about the townsfolk and politicians are bantered about to the laughter of the audience. Following the short fifteen-minute show the band plays lively folk tunes and everyone dances. During the evening festivities the actors and audience move to selected homes, performing at each stop. Each year the costumes become more and more outlandish and humorous. The procession that follows *comparsas* seems to grow each year, and the enthusiasm for the event is extreme. The *comparsas* and its procession often meets other bands and participants from neighboring pueblos. This gathering of people and costumes is the grand finale, a battle of the bands and giant mosh pit of jumping, dancing, costumed revelers. The raging bands and dancers combine for a frantic show of costumes and energetic musical sparring.

A word to the wise, while participating in the *comparsas,* if you are with a female companion who is not from Mexico, you might keep an eye on her, as you might lose her to male dancers from all ages. She might be swept away into oblivion, and most certainly she'll be lost for the evening.

With the influx of tourists into Oaxaca and the popularization of the *Día de los Muertos,* I have ventured farther from the city of Oaxaca in search of the festivities of smaller, more remote villages to find the *Muertos* ceremonies in their purest form. On All Souls Day 2001, friend and assistant Steve Giralt and I drove to the edge of the Sierra Madre del Sur Mountains to visit a cemetery in the small town of San Andres Zevache. I heard that many people would be in the cemetery that day. We arrived to find the cemetery almost deserted, although we did meet a farmer, Alfredo Perez Mafias, who asked what we were doing. After I explained my project to him, he told us to follow him. He walked us into a field of marigolds surrounded by corn and chili pepper crops. At the end of the field was a large tree, and under that tree were two men reading the Bible, eating tamales, and drinking *mescal.* Indeed they were engaging the good spirits of the Good Word and drink. They insisted that we have tamales and *mescal* while they talked of the virtues of God and the *Día de los Muertos.* I photographed them singing and reading the Bible under the tree that morning. We eventu-

ally were invited to visit their homes to meet their families, who were surprised yet excited to see us.

I have been traveling to Mexico since 1982 and have met many people throughout southern Mexico. I do not stand alone in suggesting that Oaxaca is the soul and artistic spirit of Mexico. The city and region always embrace the arts and festivals of the spirit. It is the people's enthusiasm for life and for death that has drawn me to Oaxaca for the past twenty-two years. I will continue to photograph the *Día de los Muertos* and to study the people of Oaxaca in celebration of the *Muertos.* Once you've become part of this ritual and participated in this tradition, I believe your soul will forever be bonded to the experience and the desire to return will become stronger. In a sense you've become part of a family, and, as Ward Albro says, "family ties do not die."

Denis Defibaugh
May 2004

Sand Paintings in the Zocalo Oaxaca

INTRODUCTION

FOR FIFTEEN YEARS I HAVE BEEN visiting Oaxaca during the period of the *Día de los Muertos.* From humble *jacales* (huts) on the side of a mountain to elegant Victorian homes, the people of Oaxaca welcomed me. They shared their *pan de muertos, chocolate, mole, tamales,* and more than a little of their *mescal* with me. Even more, they readily shared their experiences, telling not only how they practiced the rituals of the Day of the Dead but what it meant to them and to their families.

Oaxaca is a poor state, one of the poorest in Mexico. It is also an area of incredible physical beauty and is one of the most heavily indigenous states in Mexico, with many Indian languages and cultures. Oaxaca is the richest state in Mexico in production of folk art, and the fine art scene is also blossoming there. Colorful Indian markets abound. Major archeological sites attract visitors. Many of the churches and public buildings represent some of the finest examples of Spanish colonial architecture. Oaxacan cuisine has come to be praised in many different regions and countries. With all this, when asked why I keep going back to Oaxaca, I never hesitate to reply, "the people."

The Day of the Dead, in some ways, brings out the best in the people. I call this period "a celebration of life," and I have been fortunate to share this celebration many times with many people. Some of the finest moments for me have come from sharing my experiences with the people of Oaxaca with an outstanding photographer, Denis Defibaugh. We have not always been in Oaxaca together, but we have had some memorable times there. Denis had his share of all the food and drink mentioned above. He has spent countless hours in the markets of the central valleys, photographing the life of those markets in a unique manner. His photos taken in the homes and in the cemeteries capture the essence of *Muertos* as no others I have ever seen. Denis followed numerous parades through the Etla

Valley, and his photos of those give the viewer a real feeling of the excitement of the *comparsas*. I do not think there is any aspect of the Day of the Dead in the central valleys of Oaxaca that Denis did not experience and photograph.

Día de los Muertos in Oaxaca—a marvelous time—and here—marvelous photographs.

IT IS LATE AFTERNOON ON NOVEMBER 4 and the crowds are beginning to develop in and around the municipal cemetery in San Antonino Castillo de Velasco. San Antonino, located in the municipality of Ocotlán de Juárez, about thirty miles from the city of Oaxaca, is known to many for its brilliant *artesania*. What is called a "Mexican dress" in the United States, or perhaps a "Oaxaca dress" by somewhat more knowledgeable buyers, is in reality a dress from San Antonino, made by a handful of Zapotec seamstresses living and working there. While the ceramics from nearby Ocotlán may receive more international attention, ceramic artists from San Antonino continue to pioneer in the same colorful style. And the art of creating items with dried flowers, the *flor immortal*, has also long been practiced in San Antonino. Few realize that Oaxaca's famed Christmas season celebration, "the night of the radishes," also features a contest of scenes created with the *flor immortal.*

But what probably draws the most attention to San Antonino Castillo de Velasco is the presence in and around the town of incredible flowers, mostly commercially grown. And at no time in the year does the vibrant beauty of San Antonino's flowers burst forth as in the time of the *Día de los Muertos,* the season of the Day of the Dead in late October and early November. The cemetery is awash with the brilliant magenta *cresta de gallo* (coxcomb) blossoms. The locally harvested *cresta de gallo* overshadows the traditional flower of *Muertos,* the *cempusuchil,* or marigold, although this flower, too, is present in abundance. Also lending color to the scene, in ample quantities, are calla lilies *(cartuchos),* roses, gladiolas, and baby's breath. Fresh flowers are used in decorating the individual gravesites for several days, meaning many have been replaced. Even the piles of discarded flowers against the back wall have their own beauty.

The townspeople began to arrive about 5:00 P.M.—the women in colorful dress and elegant jewelry, the men in more simple attire, although the starched shirts indicate the special nature of the day. Even earlier, the vendors set up outside the front wall of the *panteón* (cemetery) and across the roadway from the main entrance. They will be busy all evening, preparing and selling a wide variety of food and drink—*molotes* with potato, *quesadillas* with the famed Oaxaca *quesillo* (cheese) and other fried or grilled specialties. Ice cream and *dulces regionales* (local candies) are in great demand. *Refrescos,* the carbonated beverages so popular all over Mexico, are widely sold but perhaps not as widely as the *aguas*—drinks of *tuna* (the fruit of the cactus plant), *limón,* or other fresh fruit.

As with any significant event in Oaxaca, there is always a *banda,* in this case a municipal band, playing on the elevated walkway in front of the cemetery. The members of the San Antonino town council *(ayundamiento* or *cabildo),* who made this celebration part of their official business, listen approvingly as they pass the brandy *Presidente* around their semi-circle of chairs In contrast to the rousing brass band music just outside the cemetery entrance, inside two violins pour out Zapotec funeral music.

As the evening goes on, families gather around their gravesites. The tombs, above the ground, are elaborately decorated with floral designs in packed sand, a labor of several days. Some families are putting finishing touches on these ephemeral works of art. All await the priest who will come to bless each site. He must come soon as the cemetery is not lighted, and the only candles used are in small niches at the foot of each tomb to guide the visiting spirits of the deceased back to their resting places.

But wait a minute! This is November 4th. The official national holiday for the *Día de los Muertos* is November 2nd. In the liturgical calendar of the Catholic Church, November 1st is All Saints Day and November 2nd is All Souls Day. The tour guides and other "experts" on Mexico tell us that the *animas* (souls) of *angelitos* (dead children) return on October 31st and the adults come twenty-four hours later as the children leave. The souls of the adults depart on November 2nd. Many handsome books featuring the Day of the Dead in Oaxaca are illustrated with numerous photos of the all-night, candle-lit observances in the cemetery of Xoxocotlán, on the edge of Oaxaca City and not far from the almost candle-free *panteón* in San Antonino. Virtually every cemetery in the state and the altars in the homes feature the aroma of incense burning, the widely used *copal*, a resin from the same tree used for most of the Oaxacan wood carvings. After days and nights in Oaxacan homes and cemeteries in San Antonino, you quickly notice if there is no incense in the air in other places.

As the *Día de los Muertos* has become more widely known not only throughout Mexico but also in the United States, popular literature about the traditions has increased dramatically. Unfortunately, awareness has not always led to understanding, and too much concentration on some of the more exotic aspects of the Day of the Dead has further distorted understanding.

The celebration in San Antonino makes clear that every statement about the *Día de los Muertos* in Oaxaca and other parts of Mexico must be qualified. Although some general customs prevail throughout Oaxaca, the celebration differs from place to place.

The observance of this special event evolves from year to year, particularly because of increasing interest in the importance of this unique indigenous Mexican celebration as a boon to tourism.

Ward S. Albro

ONE:

Death in Pre- and Post-Columbian Mexico

DEATH RITUALS WERE VITALLY important to pre-Colombian societies. The contents of tombs, uncovered at various archeological sites, have given much primary information about the life of these societies, along with the early Spanish accounts of the native practices. There is a Nahuatl, or even Aztec, bias to much of the knowledge that has been developed over time, since the Spaniards concentrated their attention in the Valley of Mexico. Moreover, the Aztecs themselves had spread their beliefs and absorbed other groups in their own conquests.

In these Indian societies a belief in an afterlife was universal. How a person died had a direct bearing on where in the

Gates to the *Panteón,*
Tlacochahuayo

afterlife the "soul" would reside, with favored positions given to warriors who died in battle and women who died in childbirth. All indigenous groups had fiestas devoted to recognizing the importance of the *antepasados,* or ancestors, in everyday life. These fiestas involved offerings of both food and flowers. The major festivals honoring the dead with offerings came in the ninth and tenth months, as designated by the Aztec calendar. In the polytheistic beliefs of ancient Mexico, the dead interacted with various gods on several levels. Offerings made to the dead were designed, at least in part, to encourage these spirits to act on behalf of the living with the gods. As these were agricultural societies, the months set aside for the fiestas for the dead coincide with the harvest season, generally late October. If the harvest was good, it was natural that the offerings might be a form of expressing gratitude. If the harvest was bad, the offerings would be in the nature of pleas that the spirits try to influence the gods for more help next year.

When the Spaniards came to Mexico they brought with them their own ideas about death and an afterlife. Spanish Catholicism had evolved over centuries, of course, and had shared the concerns of Catholics in general regarding the continuation of what were considered "pagan" practices. Although offerings to and for the dead seemed to be common to all cultures, what the Church thought to be "ancestor worship" was seen as incompatible with Christian beliefs. By the ninth century the Roman Catholic Church adopted November 1st as All Saints Day, a day given over to all the "unknown saints who did not have a special day set aside." All Souls Day came later, not officially adopted into the liturgical calendar until the thirteenth century. November 2nd was the day set aside to pray for all the souls in purgatory. The Church may have been slow to officially designate All Souls Day, which had been informally practiced for some years, because of concern over the "ancestor worship" question.

Spanish Catholic missionaries enjoyed remarkable success in Mexico from the beginning. The Indians quickly converted to Christianity, but that conversion in most cases meant incorporating Christianity into their existing religion. In the polytheism of indigenous Mexico, new gods, who proved their strength in subduing the Aztecs and others, found ready acceptance in the pantheon. In other cases, acceptance of

Christianity led to identifying elements of Christianity with native religions. John the Baptist, identified with Tlaloc, the rain god, remains the object of devotion in many parts of Indian Mexico. Some of the success of the Catholic Church came from the ability of missionary leaders to adapt to local practices. Finding some of the funeral and burial practices similar to their own, with festivals honoring the dead coming mostly in October, it was natural for the Spanish churchmen to incorporate aspects of indigenous beliefs into an accord with All Saints Day and All Souls Day.

For the Zapotec people in Oaxaca, this has meant that over time many of the traditions of Catholicism have simply been incorporated into their ancient beliefs. While not always coinciding with the dates of the liturgical calendar, as the example of San Antonino makes clear, the concept of a Catholic identity became part of the essentially indigenous practices of the *Día de los Muertos* The thoroughness of this syncretism was illustrated by a resident of the city of Oaxaca. Speaking at length and with obvious knowledge, this man explained the essentially Zapotec nature of the *Día de los Muertos* in Oaxaca. After he convincingly explained why and how the celebration is and always has been Zapotec, someone asked, "Do you put up an altar?" "No," he replied, "I am a Protestant."

Panteón, Xoxocotlán,
GMI Gravestone

Panteón, Xoxocotlán,
Candle Cross

Family, *Panteón,*
Tlacochahuayo

Candle Light Portrait,
Panteón, Atzompa

Gravestones and Candles,
Panteón, Atzompa

Panteón, Xoxocotlán,
Two Girls and Family

12

Elvira, *Panteón,*
San Antonino
Castillo de Velasco

14

Flower Contest, San
Antonino Castillo de
Valesco

Two Brothers,
Panteón, San
Antonino Castillo
de Velasco

Crosses, *Panteón*,
San Antonino
Castillo de
Velasco

Red Dress and Marigolds,
Panteón, Ayoquezco de
Aldama

Girl with Flowers and
Taco, *Panteón,*
Ayoquezco de Aldama

Maurilia Bracamontes
Mónjaraz Family, *Panteón,*
Oaxaca

Children Playing,
Panteón, Oaxaca

Flowers, *Panteón,* San
Martin Tilcajete

Man with One Flower,
Panteón, San Martin
Tilcajete

Panteón, Ayoquezco
de Aldama

25

Carrying the Cross,
Panteón, Oaxaca

Bernarda, *Panteón*, San
Antonino Castillo de
Velasco

Preparing the
Atzompa
Cemetery

Children's Games,
Panteón, San Felipe
del Agua

Antonino Alonso Santiago Family, *Panteón*, San Antonino Castillo

Morning Candles, *Panteón*, San Felipe del Agua

Mazunte *Panteón*

Band in the *Panteón*, Oaxaca

INRI with Flowers, *Panteón*, Teotitlán del Valle

Walking through the *Panteón*, San Antonino Castillo de Velasco

Virgin of Guadalupe Statue, *Panteón*, San Juan Zabache

Family Portait at the Grave, *Panteón*, Teotitlán del Valle

TWO:

Indian Markets and Muertos

Lanterns and Masks, Mercado de Abastos, Oaxaca

STILL WITHSTANDING THE INTRUSIONS of the Wal-Marts of the world, the indigenous markets of Oaxaca survive and serve local needs and also offer unique experiences to visitors, both national and international. Virtually every city, town, and village has its special market day. Among the largest and most visited are the Friday market in Ocotlán, the Sunday market in Tlacolula, and the sprawling, huge *mercado de abastos* in Oaxaca City. While the Oaxaca market is open every day, Saturday is the special market day that brings vendors and buyers from all over the central valleys of Oaxaca. In every case, the market day immediately before the Day of the Dead is generally the busiest day of the year.

Every market has the usual items found year round: fruits and vegetables; herbs and spices; meats; fish; bread; nuts; chocolate; flowers; clothing; dishes and cooking utensils; tools, and so forth. Oaxaca also produces special items. For example, in the Tlacolula market and others in the Tlacolula Valley numerous stalls offer Zapotec weavings from Teotitlán del Valle and other weaving centers in the valley. Tlacolula is also considered the most authentic Zapotec market in the central valley, as is well illustrated by the traditional clothing worn by the numerous indigenous women both buying and selling in the market. In the Etla Valley, to the north of Oaxaca City, abundant fruits and vegetables attest to the richer lands and adequate water in that valley. In markets in the third valley that comes to merge into Oaxaca City and make up what are often called the central valleys, the Big Valley or the Ocotlán Valley, the black pottery, backstrap weavings, and elaborate blouses and dresses are the unique products of the area.

The *Día de los Muertos* brings a very special feeling to every market. First, there are the items that will be used in the altars in the homes. The essence of the celebration is in the homes and with the families. In the construction of altars in many areas, an arch of sugar cane stalks, sold in most markets, is used as the backdrop. Flowers form an important part of every altar. The normal section of markets given over to flowers is not big enough for the needs of this season, so usually there are special sections with the *cempasuchil, cresta de gallo*, and many other varieties. Most altars are put up at the last minute so it is essential that the market contains enough of every item at its freshest. A special flower market is held in Miahuatlán de Porfirio Díaz, about halfway between the city of Oaxaca and the Pacific Coast. Most Oaxacans do not have to go too far to get their goods for *Muertos*, but the popularity of this market, held the afternoon and evening before most areas begin their observances, attests to the central role flowers play in the celebration.

Other everyday items in the market take on special meaning and appearance during the season. Citrus fruit would be normally stacked in neat pyramids. Since such fruit is also used as decoration on the altars, the citrus in the Day of the Dead market has stems and leaves attached. Other fruits and vegetables common to Oaxaca include jicama, *tejocotes*, and *manzanitas* (small apples used in desserts as well as altar decorations).

Bread is everywhere, the famed *pan de muertos,* a symbol of life in the time of death. This egg-yolk bread is baked in round loaves of varying sizes. Baked into the bread is a pasta-like hard dough, shaped as a colored image of the Christ child, an angel, or other religious figure. These figures are also sold at the market for those who bake their own bread, and nowadays, besides the traditional religious figures, the latest movie or television cartoon character will be available for a modern addition to the very traditional bread. Since the bread is used in every altar, shared with family and friends, and eaten with Oaxaca's renowned chocolate, it is available in great abundance in every market. In the central market in Oaxaca City, master bakers from Santo Domingo Tomaltepec, a nearby village famous for its bakers and bakeries, often are brought into the city to work, staying for three or four days baking the bread. Some towns are well known for distinctive breads. Many outsiders come to Zaachila to buy the elaborately decorated bread baked in that pecan tree-surrounded town, which also lays claim to having been the last center of the Zapotec world. *Pan de muertos* from Mitla, less colorful but more intricately decorated, is also known all over the central valleys.

Market items that might not be thought of as *Muertos* related include clothing, dishes, and cooking utensils. Yet, these goods are significant because families make every effort to have new clothes, new dishes, and new pots and pans to honor their deceased family members and to begin a new cycle of life. The new clothing becomes part of the *ofrenda* on the altar, for the pleasure of the returning spirit but to be used by other family members later. The cooking utensils and the dishes are used to prepare and serve the special meals that are an essential part of the celebration and will be used throughout the year to come. Given the relative poverty of Oaxaca, dishes, pots, and pans found in the public market tend to be very inexpensive.

Markets also now include special sections given over to *Muertos.* In the central market in the city of Oaxaca this section gets larger every year. Besides serving the needs of the entire central valleys, it has become a tourist attraction. Here one can find merchandise from the sacred to the silly. The sacred would include images of saints and Jesus and Mary, which are displayed on home altars and sometimes taken to gravesites in the cemetery. A particular favorite is the Virgin of Soledad, the *patrona* of Oaxaca. In the same area of the market

38

Red Priest,
Mercado de
Abastos, Oaxaca

are numerous stalls featuring an infinite number of candles in all shapes and sizes. Candles are prominent in the home altars and in many cemeteries.

Numerous toys are sold in the market, many featuring the theme of death through the use of the now familiar *calavera*. These skeleton figures are involved in all manner of activities in the creations of the Oaxaca artisans. Among such items, which are obviously of modern origin, are robed pallbearers, made of paper with garbanzo-bean heads, carrying a casket. These are seen on all kinds of altars and throughout the cemeteries and seem to fit in with the other skeleton figures made of many different materials. However, these figures date back to the nineteenth century as typical decorations for the Day of the Dead. In many ways, there has been a seamless merger of the modern with the traditional in this celebration.

The smell of incense, typically *copal,* fills the air in the *Muertos* section of the market. Many parts of the *mercado* sell incense and the three- or four-legged stone incense burners, in which samples are burned to attract the customers. These will be placed in front of many home altars and are common in most cemeteries.

Candy of various types, the *dulces regionales* of Oaxaca, plays a prominent role in the Day of the Dead. Sugar skulls are sold in all sizes in the market. At many stalls, the vendor will personalize a skull with the name of an individual. Candy makers in Oaxaca have made and sold sugar skulls for generations, although the techniques for the more elaborately decorated skulls may have been imported from Puebla. Some people contend that the sugar skull is a substitute for the actual skulls that were common on altars in years gone by. The ancient indigenous practice of digging up and cleaning the bones of ancestors did not survive the coming of European Catholicism. Many other candies are sold in the markets in Oaxaca, most featuring the *calavera* or skeleton motif in one way or another. In the *abastos* market in Oaxaca City separate stalls appear in the *Muertos* section. In markets in smaller towns and villages the weekly vendors of the *dulces regionales* turn most of their efforts and production over to the candy of the season.

One of the most important areas of the market associated with the Day of the Dead is that where Oaxacans buy their ingredients for the special *Muertos* meals. First and foremost is the *mole negro* that will be served with turkey, if the family can afford it, or with chicken as the main meal of the day, usually on November 2nd. Prepared mole is for sale in the market, but stall and after stall features the forty or fifty ingredients that go into the complicated and labor-intensive making of Oaxacan *mole*. Chocolate, of course, the chocolate that gives the distinctive flavor, and the herbs and spices, the essential chiles, onions, garlic, tomatoes, raisins, nuts, and on and on. In the *Muertos* market additional bread is sold. Other stalls sell *calabaza* (squash) as well as the squash blossoms to be used in soups. *Manzanitas,* the little apples sold for decorative purposes, are also used in preparing a typical dessert. Oaxacan tamales are an important part of the meals, and banana leaves to wrap the traditional tamales and the *masa* to be filled, usu-ally with *mole,* are sold. In the market in Teotitlán del Valle, the weaving center, the traditional tamale of this season is wrapped in corn leaves instead of banana.

The market shows growing evidence of the impact of United States-style Halloween celebrations. Stalls are devoted to masks of all types, from monsters to cartoon characters. Political leaders are parodied in rubber masks, two of the favorite being the currents presidents of both the United States and Mexico. There are also costumes for the children. Witches and goblins are foreign to the traditions of the Day of the Dead in Oaxaca but are gaining ground every year. The indigenous markets of Oaxaca tell much of the past, present, and future of this most important time of the year.

42

Brother and Sister, Mercado
de Abastos, Oaxaca

Toy Skeleton Still Life, Oaxaca

School Celebration, Zaachila

Flowers for
the Altar,
Mercado de
Abastos,
Oaxaca

46

Poultry Vendors,
Mercado,
Ocatlán de
Morelos

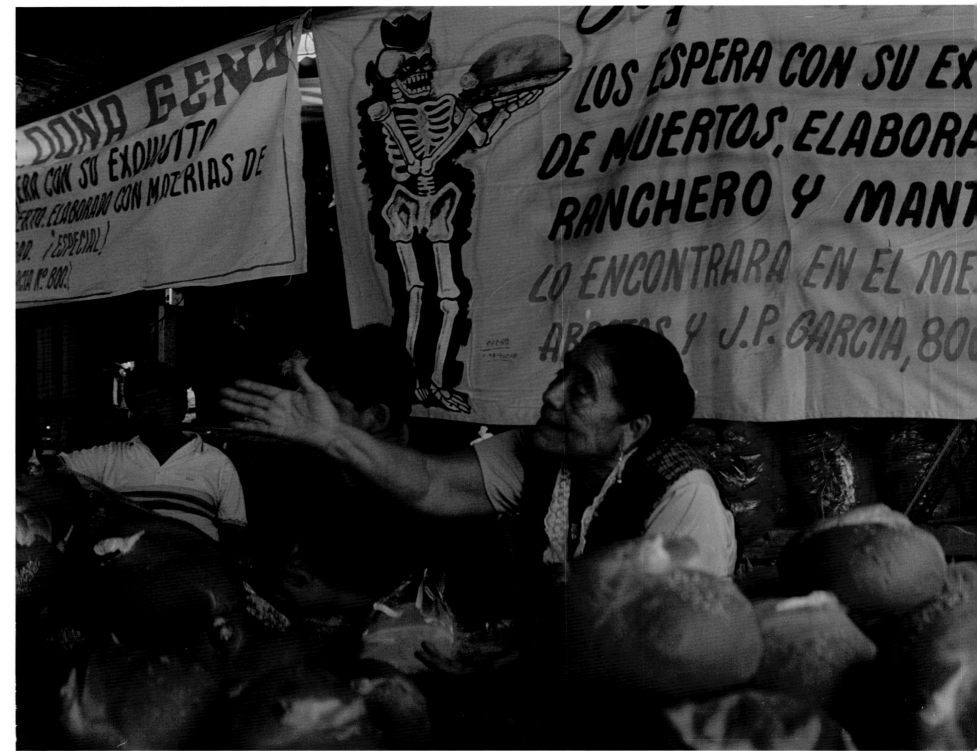

48

Bread for the
Dead, Mercado
de Abastos,
Oaxaca

Etla *Comparsas,*
Bell Costume

THREE:

Death on Parade

SOME SEE A TREND FOR MORE
Halloween-style celebrations in the evolution of the *comparsas*
in the Etla Valley, which take place on the night of November
1st. The Etla area, to the north of Oaxaca City, is the richest
of the three valleys that make up the central valley of Oaxaca.
A number of foreigners have homes in the area, along with
upper-class Oaxacans. The land yields two crops a year for the
farmers in the area, giving them a great advantage over the drier
Tlacolula and Ocotlán valleys. A unique form of street theater
has developed in several of the communities of the Etla area.
Called the *comparsas,* it is sometimes referred to as a form of
"Trick or Treat" but it is much more than that.

Comparsas
Stiltmen, San
Augustín Etla

Costumes at the
Cathedral, Oaxaca

The *comparsas* is part theater, part dance, and a good part simply fun. The performers are all males, even though some of the roles are female. From very young children to adults, the participants themselves pay for elaborate costumes. There are several stock characters, including a priest, a landowner, his wife who becomes a widow, the *mayordomo,* and several other characters with speaking parts. Then there are many dancing devils of all sizes without speaking parts. All leave from a meeting place and follow a *banda*, a brass band hired for the entire night from another village, to the town square. Here a play is enacted which involves the struggle over the soul of a deceased man. Much of the dialog is ad libbed, although the leading characters have usually participated in the performance for several years and have worked their way up to coveted roles.

While increasing numbers of tourist groups attend the *comparsas,* the performance is not what you would call "tourist friendly." There is no amplification for the speaking parts. There is no translation. The humor is based primarily on "in-jokes" involving various national, state, and, particularly, local public figures. After the "drama" comes to a conclusion, all the actors and the devils dance wildly, mainly by jumping up

and down to the music of the *banda.* They follow the band through the night, stopping at certain houses in the community where the "trick-or-treat" aspect comes out. Here the players recite humorous satirical verses about the residents of the house, until all are invited in for a "treat." It might be bread and chocolate for the younger participants and maybe *mescal* for the older ones. This goes on all night and often results in tired children and inebriated adults by the time the *comparsas* concludes on the morning of November 2nd. In earlier years, the homes were chosen at random. Nowadays, they are pre-selected, and the occupants know the *comparsas* is coming. The humor also tends to be less harsh or "biting" than it was earlier.

While the traditional *comparsas* continues to be performed and to attract some outside interest, more attention has shifted to a simplified version carried out in several towns in the Etla Valley on the other side of the *autopista.* Here the participants do not act out elaborate plays but follow bands, again hired for the night, from town to town. Some of the home-made costumes are incredibly complex and show great imagination. They also have little relevance to *Muertos.* The parading dancers, again all male, followed by many of their fellow townspeople and other spectators, go to designated homes to dance wildly to the band's music. Ultimately, they end up at a town square and perform an abbreviated play in front of the church. Groups of dancers and their *bandas* sometimes come together on the road or in the towns, and it is almost like a battle of the bands. These parades are great fun and attract many followers, including an increasing number of tourists.

There have been attempts to import this newer version of the *comparsas* into Oaxaca City, but it does not work as well outside the Etla Valley. The costumes, however, do show the increasing influence of Halloween traditions imposing themselves on the *Día de los Muertos* in Oaxaca. Some might argue that more than Halloween, the *comparsas* is another way Mexicans "laugh" at death.

Performance Group,
Oaxaca

Etla *Comparsas,*
Diablo and Horse

Etla *Comparsas,*
Tuba Battle

Etla *Comparsas,*
Trombone Player

The Spirit Returns,
Oaxaca

Oaxaca City *Comparsas,*
Woman with Pearls

Etla *Comparsas*,
Che

Etla *Comparsas*,
Mosh Pit

Etla *Comparsas,*
Mosh Pit

Etla *Comparsas*,
Mohawk Doll

Winged Monster in Suit, Etla *Comparsas*

Diablo Child, Etla *Comparsas*

Chef and Boy, Etla Comparsas

Fat Face Couple, Etla Comparsas

Skeleton and Fat Man, Etla *Comparsas*

Filemón Donkey, Etla *Comparsas*

Playboy
Comparsas,
Oaxaca

FOUR:

Observances in the Homes

DESPITE IMMENSE PUBLICITY, government promotions, and organized tours to the cemeteries, the Day of the Dead in Oaxaca remains essentially a family celebration, centered in the home. Although there are sixteen distinct indigenous languages spoken in Oaxaca, with many additional dialects, and a corresponding number of indigenous groups, the *Día de los Muertos* in the central valleys of Oaxaca is primarily Zapotec in origin. Even with the common origins, there are often significant differences from village to village.

Common to all areas is the construction in the home of an altar with an *ofrenda* (offering) in honor of deceased family

Home of Irene
Aguilar, Altar, Jesús
and the Skeleton,
Ocotlán de Morelos

Home of Josefina
Aguilar Altar,
Rambo, Ocotlán de
Morelos

members. In every case it is the "dead of memory," family members who were known to at least some members of the living family. The physical setting of the altar may vary considerably from one area to another. For example, in Teotitlán del Valle and many other towns in the Tlacolula Valley, altars are built into the homes when they are constructed. Generally, a long counter across the narrow end of a family room is used as an altar all the time. The contents change for the observance of *Muertos.* In Ocotlán and other towns in the big valley, tables are placed in the home specifically to hold the *ofrenda.* This practice is probably most common throughout the central valleys of Oaxaca. Altars are usually constructed on October 31st and taken down on November 2nd, although in recent years the tendency has been to keep the altars around a little longer.

The altar is framed with sugar cane stalks from which may hang various fruits and flowers. Often the smaller fruits are strung together. Flowers are displayed on the altar and all around it, particularly the marigolds, or *cempasuchil.* The coxcomb is also frequently used. Depending on the economic circumstances and the physical location of the families involved, flowers are purchased in the market or from any of the numerous flower stands or gathered by hand from the fields. Fresh flowers are usually added each day the *ofrenda* is maintained.

On the altar itself some or all of the following are displayed:

Pictures of saints and other religious figures.

Framed photographs of the person or persons being honored.

Candles.

Chocolate and peanuts.

Many loaves of the *pan de muertos,* the special bread of the season.

Additional fruits and vegetables.

Prepared foods such as *mole, tamales, calabaza,* or special favorites of the person or persons being honored.

Carbonated beverages in bottles, particularly the ever-present Coca-Cola.

Bottles of beer and *mescal,* if appropriate for the recognized *antepasado.* Packages of cigarettes.

Items of new clothing.

Dishes that will be used in the major meal served on the Day of the Dead.

Sugar skulls and other candies and toys featuring *calaveras* and other symbols of the Day of the Dead.

More flowers and candles are on the floor in front of the altar, along with incense in the special burner. Some of the flowers are often arranged in intricate designs on the floor.

If there are children, or *angelitos,* being honored, the altars will be somewhat different. In the central valleys of Oaxaca, this might be done in any of three manners: a separate smaller altar might be set up; items related to the children might be included on the main altar and then removed before the arrival of the spirits of the adults; or a special section of the altar may be given over to the *angelitos.* The latter is common when the altar is long and built into the wall, as is done in the Tlacolula Valley. The content, obviously, of an *ofrenda* for children is different—fewer spicy foods, no alcohol, and more toys and other items relating directly to the lives of the children being honored.

The belief is that the *ánimas,* or souls, of the deceased return to share a day with the living. Because the almost universal belief is that the souls of the *angelitos* return twenty-four hours before the adults and depart before the latter's arrival, the same altar with different contents might be used in some homes. People do not believe that the returning souls will eat the food on the altars, but they do believe the *ánimas* inhale or absorb the essence of the food. After the visit of twenty-four hours the souls return to the cemetery, sometimes being escorted back. Physical presence of the remains is very important. Oaxacans in the United States, and there are many, relate their sadness if they cannot get back to Oaxaca for *Muertos.* It is impossible to celebrate the day if not physically close to the remains.

There is a strong sense of obligation in the observance of the *Día de los Muertos.* Time and again the story is told, in various forms, about the terrible tragedies that befall people who do not honor their *antepasados.* Although it is usually the same story with minor modifications, it is told as if it came from first-hand knowledge. Beyond the obligation, however, is the fact that this celebration of the dead is a strong reaffirmation of the living. By families coming together at this time, the most important days of the year for the indigenous people of Oaxaca, family ties are strengthened.

The immediate family comes together to celebrate and share this time with the souls of the deceased. More distant family, wives' family members (as the concentration in the homes is on the male line), and friends also share some of the celebration. It is common in many areas to share visits and ritual exchanges of items from the altars. A family may come to call bearing *pan de muertos*, fruit, chocolate, nuts, and the like. After sharing bread and chocolate, or maybe *mescal* and a *tamal*, the visitors depart carrying bread, fruit, chocolate, nuts, and the like from the host's altar. No visitor, family or not, leaves without being given bread and other goods. It is not even an intrusion for strangers, usually tourists, to visit during this time. No matter how humble or how elaborate, Oaxacans want to share their altars with others. In some ways, the visitors are seen as helping carry the souls home. The Zapotec culture is widely recognized as one of the most gracious and welcoming cultures in Mexico.

Most experts agree that one of the defining elements of a culture is food. Certainly food plays a major role in the celebration of the *Día de los Muertos*. In the early hours of the morning in the cemetery in Atzompa, the pottery center at the foot of Monte Albán, a native of the village currently living in California, was asked, "Did you come back for the *Muertos?*" He replied, "No, for the *mole*." Although spoken in jest, there was a good deal of truth in the reply. Oaxacans living in the United States often speak of the food they miss.

While the *pan de muertos* is all over the altars and eaten in great quantities, many times with a steaming cup or bowl of *chocolate con agua*, it is the deep chocolate-and-chile flavored *mole* that is the essential food item of the Day of the Dead in Oaxaca. The women of Oaxaca take great pride in their *moles*, sometimes even giving a competitive edge to the preparation of the sauce that smothers the turkey or chicken in the main meal of the *Muertos* season, no matter what day that might be in whatever town or village. The visitor is often compelled to sample many *moles* and must be careful to praise each as the best. The dark *mole* is also used in the preparation of the distinctive Oaxacan tamales. Men, women, and even children will sip a little of Oaxaca's major alcoholic drink, *mescal*, on the grounds that it helps in the digestion of the rich, heavy mole.

Although no food involves the time and effort of the preparation of the *mole*, with its myriad ingredients, most of the food preparation is labor intensive. Yet, this, too, contributes to the strengthening of family ties during the celebration of the Day of the Dead. Several generations of women will usually be found in the kitchen, whether the kitchen is indoors or outdoors, making tortillas and *tamales*, boiling the chickens, creating the *mole*, and preparing the other dishes spe-cial to both Oaxaca and to the season. The sharing of food, both in the preparation and the eating, in major meals at home or at a picnic in the cemetery, contributes to an appreciation of family.

The experiences in the homes in the central valleys of Oaxaca illustrate over and over what some observers find ironic or confusing. This observance of death is in reality a cel-ebration of life, with a recognition that death is, ultimately, part of life. Death does not end the family but strengthens the ties that hold families together.

Altar with Religious
Paintings, Ocotlán de
Morelos

Alfredo Pérez Matías
Family Altar, San
Andrés Zabache

Home of Irene Aguilar,
Señor y Dador de Vida
Altar, Ocotlán de
Morelos

Home Altar, Santa
Cantalina Mines

Altar Detail, Home of
Isaac Vásquez,
Teotitlán del Valle

Still Life of Candy,
Ocotlán de Morelos

Altar, Home of
Aurora Sosa,
Mitla

Altar Portrait with
Angel, Hosteria de
Alcala, Oaxaca

FIVE:

Public and Commercial Celebrations

Local governments obviously play the most prominent role in capitalizing on the tourist potential of the Day of the Dead, but they are certainly not alone. It was, after all the national government that took this largely indigenous celebration observed in parts of central and southern Mexico and made it a national holiday. This has attracted increasing numbers of tourists in recent years. In addition to the many foreign tourists who come to the *Día de los Muertos,* many Mexicans from Mexico City north want to see what this national holiday celebration is all about. It obviously was more than a *Posada calavera.*

The national government has not played a role in the Oaxacan celebrations comparable to that in much of

Zócalo Political
Altar, Oaxaca

Michoacán. Although the *Día de los Muertos* observance at the island village of Janitzio on Lake Pátzcuaro may well be the most famous and most visited of all such celebrations, the activities in many of the other villages around the lake have been in essence created by government agencies. In Oaxaca, the authentic celebration of the Day of the Dead has always existed in the villages, and the practices are being modified as they are brought into the city.

For years local communities and schools have had altar contests. The argument has generally been made that such contests are designed to preserve traditions rather than to attract tourists. Many such contests are indeed held in out-of-the-way villages that have never seen a tourist. But when these contests develop in places such as the city of Oaxaca, the intent becomes less clear.

The city of Oaxaca has sponsored exhibits of altars from the various regions of Oaxaca. These altars were first set up in the city cemetery and more recently in the patio of the city hall. Foreign tourists visited the altars but with nothing of the organization or interest that might accompany trips to the cemeteries at Xoxocotlán. The interest seemed to be greater among Oaxacans themselves, lending weight to the idea that preservation of traditions might be foremost.

The city did sponsor events called *muerteada* for a number of years, which was basically an attempt to bring aspects of the special celebrations of the Etla Valley into the city. Scheduling street theater activities and costumed parades was of limited success as the festive activities on the streets of Oaxaca, not uncommon at any time of the year, work best when there is a sense of spontaneity.

Public buildings throughout Oaxaca always have an altar for *Muertos* as do any number of civic and cultural groups. Historic figures may be honored on these altars. Perhaps the founder of an organization will be honored or a library might recognize an author. Sometimes, particular groups or causes are designated. In recent years in Oaxaca victims of AIDS have appeared on altars. Battered women were featured on another Day of the Dead display. Political statements sometimes appear on altars on the streets.

Art galleries often schedule openings of shows featuring *Muertos* themes. The galleries and art students at the local universities create elaborate public representations for the Day of the Dead. This also involves the city government as many such creations are located on public spaces.

The many shops selling artisan products make use of their knowledge and inventory to put together exceptional altars and other displays. Almost every shop in the valleys of Oaxaca will have some sort of display. The large hotels and restaurants can be counted on to present elegant altars. Many contract with some of Oaxaca's most famous artists and artisans to construct their altars. Since schools are in session in October and November, altar contests in the schools are almost universal. In the lower grades, parties that bear close resemblance to Halloween take place. That foreshadows a trend in the development of the Day of the Dead that seems inevitable.

Political Altar for
Digna Ochoa,
Zócalo Oaxaca

Protest Altar for
Bartolomé Chávez
Salas, Zócalo,
Oaxaca

94

Mortician's Family
Altar, Ocotlán de
Morelos

SIX:

People of Oaxaca

Altar, Home of
Antonio Gonzales
Vásquez, Teotitlán
del Valle

Francisco Hernández
Cruz Family Altar San
Martín Tilcajete

98

Altar, Home of
Mariana Reyes, Colonia
Moctezuma, Oaxaca

Skulls on a Stick,
Oaxaca

Candy Makers, Three
Generations of
Martínez Family,
Oaxaca

Silvia Patino Gómez
and Candy Skulls,
Ocotlán de Morelos

Biviana Alavez
Hipolito Candle
Maker, Teotitlán
del Valle

Timeteo López
Godinez, Artisan of
Flor Imortal, San
Antonino Castillo
de Velasco

Bakery Owners,
Santo Domingo
Comaltepec

Master Baker of
pan de muertos,
Santo Domingo
Comaltepec

Flowers for the
Cemetery, San Martín
Tilcajete

Mescal Maestro,
Santo Cantalina
Mines

Singing Lawyer,
San Andrés
Zabache

Geraldo Flores,
Muertos Ring,
Oaxaca

ACKNOWLEDGEMENTS

WITH LOVE I WOULD LIKE TO THANK the angel Elaine Defibaugh for her continued support and enthusiasm for my work.

Ward Albro introduced me to the *Día de los Muertos*. I am grateful for his text for the book, his incredible knowledge of Mexico that he generously shares with everyone, and for his willingness to drink *mescal* with me before 9:00 in the morning. I am thankful that he was willing to put together the major grant proposals for the "Family Ties Do Not Die, *the Día de los Muertos*" project, and early exhibitions.

I have received support from a number of organizations and individuals that I would like to recognize. Peter Lebowitz of Agfa has generously supported this project from the beginning. The Texas Committee for the Humanities for their early exhibition grants. Rochester Institute of Technology's College of Imaging Arts and Sciences has continually supported the project with FEAD grants and exhibition opportunities. The Connor Museum at Texas A&M Kingsville has provided invaluable advice and exhibition help.

I owe a debt of gratitude for the encouragement and ongoing guidance of CIAS Dean Joan Stone and Photographic Arts Department Chair William DuBois. The School of Photographic Arts and Science faculty has never failed to provide any and all types of assistance during the many years of this project. In particular I thank Doug Manchee, Allen Vogel, Guenther Cartwright, John Retallack, Howard LeVant, Elaine O'Neil David Pankow, Amelia Hugill-Fontanel, and Patti Ambrogi for always being on my side. In addition, I owe much gratitude to Therese Mulligan for editing pictures and text.

Many thanks to Bruce Ian Meader for his design ideas for my Day of the Dead images, and James Colby for his support and insight into my photography. I am also grateful for John

Latimer's guidance and Melissa Olen's dedication in preparation of image files.

Many people have helped to coordinate this project in Mexico. Pedro Javier Torres Hernández was an invaluable guide with his introductions to the artisans, festivals, and storytellers of the *Día de los Muertos.* Lucero Topete of the *Instituto Cultural Oaxaca* provided cultural insight to the *Muertos.*

Thank you to Shari Brown for offering her fine abode and for her expatriate view of the festival. Obviously this project would not have come together without the cooperation of all the people that were willing to share their *Día de los Muertos* experiences through my photography.

For my mother Leota Defibaugh and brothers David and Dexter.

Denis Defibaugh

D ENIS DEFIBAUGH HAS EXPRESSED his appreciation to the many people involved in this project.

I would like to add special thanks to three people.

To Denis, who not only has become a good friend but who made me look smart for involving him with the Day of the Dead.

To Judy Alter, for her encouragement and support in making this book a reality.

And, especially, to my wife, Tot, who has given me such a great life after *Muertos.*

Ward S. Albro

DAY OF THE DEAD

For Further Reading

Andrade, Mary J. *Through the Eyes of the Soul, Day of the Dead in Mexico. A Través de los Ojos del Alma, Día de los Muertos en México.* San José, California: La Oferta Review Newspaper, Inc., 1996

A series of three books on the Day of the Dead with photos and texts by the author. The subjects are Michoacán; Mexico City, Mixquic, and Morelos; and Oaxaca. The Oaxaca volume covers the whole state.

Carmichael, Elizabeth, and Chloë Sayer. *The Skeleton at the Feast: The Day of the Dead in Mexico.* Austin: University of Texas Press, 1992

Probably still the best scholarly account, although it has relatively little on Oaxaca itself.

Ruiz, Efraín Cortés, and Beatriz Oliver Vega, Catalina Rodríguez Lazcano, Dora Sierra Carrillo, and Plácido Villanueva Pecado, *The Days of the Dead: A Mexican Tradition.* Mexico City: GV Editores, 1988

An early but still good introduction to the subject by Mexican scholars.

Garciagodoy, Juanita. *Digging the Days of the Dead: A Reading of Mexico's Dias de Muertos.* Niwot, Colorado: The University Press of Colorado, 1998

A broad, sometimes very personal account of the subject by a U.S. Spanish professor.

Greenleigh, John, and Rosalind Rosoff Beimler. *The Days of the Dead. Los Días de Muertos.* San Francisco: Collins Publishers, 1991

Greenleigh's photos and Beimler's text concentrate on central Mexico.

Suggested Children's Books

Tony Johnston, Tony, and Jeanette Winter, *Day of the Dead.* San Diego, New York, and London: Harcourt Brace and Company, 1996

Ancona, George. *Pablo Remembers: The Fiesta of the Day of the Dead.* New York: Lothrop, Lee & Shepard Books, 1993

Lasky, Kathryn, with photographs by Christopher G. Knight. *Days of the Dead.* New York: Hyperion Books for Children, 1994

Luenn, Nancy, with illustrations by Robert Chapman, *A Gift for Abuelita: Celebrating the Day of the Dead / Un regalo para Abuelita: En celebración del Día de los Muertos.* Flagstaff, Arizona: Northland Publishing Company, 1998

Krull, Kathleen, with illustrations by Enrique O. Sánchez. *Maria Molina and the Days of the Dead.* New York: Macmillan Publishing Company, 1994

Levy, Janice, with illustrations by Morella Fuenmayor. *The Spirit of Tío Fernando: A Day of the Dead Story / El espíritu de Tío Fernando: Una Historia del Día de los Muertos.* Mortin Grove, Illinois: Albert Whitman & Company, 1995

Hoyt-Goldsmith, Diane, with photographs by Lawrence Migdale. *Day of the Dead: A Mexican-American Celebration.* New York: Holiday House, 1994

The Day of the Dead / *Día de los Muertos*

Design and Illustrations by Barbara Mathews Whitehead

Set in Centaur MT

A type designed by Bruce Rogers in 1928

from an exemplar by Nicholas Jenson in 1470

3000 *Copies Printed and Bound in China by*

Everbest

2007